*ClearNotes* **Essentials**™

Notes on

AP Physics C – Electricity and Magnetism

Chand Samaratunga, PhD

ISBN: 1470188201
ISBN-13: 978-1470188207

# CONTENTS

# FORWARD

This booklet should be used as a supplement to classroom work and laboratory experiments conducted as a part of AP Physics C coursework. When definitional issues arise or there is a need to get a clear mathematical understanding of the concepts involved, this supplement should be resorted to.

A mathematics knowledge available at AP Calculus AB or C levels is sufficient to understand this booklet. Additional calculus concepts needed (line integral and surface integral) are introduced in Chapter 1.

In Chapter 2, the concept of symmetry relating to physical objects and vectors are briefly introduced. Chapters 3 and 4 comprehensively introduce the AP Physics C Electricity and Magnetism syllabus, with many real examples. Important concepts of electric potential and electric current are clearly defined without ambiguity, since these concepts often lead students astray. In Chapter 3, Coulomb's Law is introduced and shown that it comes from Gauss's Law of Electricity. Subsequently capacitance and resistance are defined, and their electric energy storage and consumption computed. For conductors, Ohm's Law is proven as a part of the calculation of its resistance.

In Chapter 4, magnetic field is defined via the Lorentz Equation. Then Ampere's Law for Steady Current is introduced and shown that it is equivalent to Biot-Savart Law. Then Faraday's Law of Electric Induction is introduced, the concept of inductance defined, and motors and generators explained.

In Chapter 5, electrical circuits are introduced, and Kirchoff's Laws are proven in terms of electric potential and electric charge conservation. Then the transient behavior of RC, RL, and LC circuits in series and in parallel are discussed. Then, the behavior of alternating current through each of R, C, and L circuit elements discussed.

In Chapter 6, Maxwell's Equations are discussed in terms of the equivalence of their integral form with Gauss's Laws, and Faraday's Law. Maxwell's modification of Ampere's Law needed to confirm with real life observations is next discussed.

Chand Samaratunga, PhD
March, 2012

# Chapter 1: SOME CALCULUS RESULTS

1. Line Vector and Functions on a Line

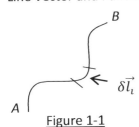

Figure 1-1

a) Consider a line of length $l$ going from a point A to another point B in space. Let us cut that line to $i$ small segments. Assume that the length of the $i$ th segment ($i = 1, 2, ...., n$) of the line connecting point A to point B is given by $\overrightarrow{\delta l_i}$. The length $\overrightarrow{\delta l_i}$ can then be assumed to be a straight line with a certain fixed direction at a point $(x_i, y_i, z_i)$ with lengths $(\delta l_{x_i}, \delta l_{y_i}, \delta l_{z_i})$ in the X, Y, and Z directions of the X-Y-Z coordinate plane. At the limit, $\overrightarrow{\delta l_i} \to 0$.

b) It is known that a function can be defined on points on a X-Y-Z coordinate plane. Hence a function can also be defined only on the set of points along a line in space, since line is simply a restriction on the X-Y-Z coordinate plane.

c) Further, a function $\vec{f}(x, y\, z)$ can be defined on the points of a line as a 3 dimensional vector given by $(f_1(x, y, z),\ f_2(x, y, z),\ f_3(x, y, z))$.

d) The magnitude of the above function at point $(x, y, z)$ is given by,

$$|\vec{f}(x, y\, z)| = \sqrt{(f_1(x, y, z))^2 + (f_2(x, y, z))^2 + (f_3(x, y, z))^2}$$  eq(1-1)

Similarly,  $|\overrightarrow{\delta l_i}| = \sqrt{(\delta l_{x_i})^2 + (\delta l_{y_i})^2 + (\delta l_{z_i})^2}$  eq(1-2)

e) A unit vector pointing in the direction of the function at point $(x, y, z)$ is given by,

$$1_{\vec{f}} = \frac{\vec{f}(x, y\, z)}{|\vec{f}(x, y\, z)|}$$  eq(1-3)

f) The scalar quantity $\vec{f}(x_i, y_i, z_i) . \overrightarrow{\delta l_i}$ is called the DOT product, and it is defined as,

$$\vec{f}(x_i, y_i, z_i).\overrightarrow{\delta l_i} = f_1(x, y, z).\delta l_{x_i} + f_2(x, y, z).\delta l_{y_i} + f_3(x, y, z).\delta l_{z_i}$$  eq(1-4)

g) It can also be shown that

$$\vec{f}(x_i, y_i, z_i).\overrightarrow{\delta l_i} = |\vec{f}(x_i, y_i, z_i)|.|\overrightarrow{\delta l_i}|.\cos(\theta_i)$$  eq(1-5)

where $\theta_i$ is the angle between the two vectors.

h) The vector quantity $\vec{f}(x_i, y_i, z_i) \times \overrightarrow{\delta l_i}$ is called the CROSS product. The direction of this vector is perpendicular to the plane containing the vectors $\vec{f}(x_i, y_i, z_i)$, and $\overrightarrow{\delta l_i}$. If the fingers of your right hand is

1

rotated from the direction of $\vec{f}(x_i, y_i, z_i)$ to $\delta\vec{l_i}$, then the thumb points in the direction of the CROSS product. (Right Hand Rule.)

$$|\vec{f}(x_i, y_i, z_i) \times \delta\vec{l_i}| = |\vec{f}(x_i, y_i, z_i)|.|\delta\vec{l_i}|.\sin(\theta_i)$$  eq(1-6)

## 2. Line Integral

A line integral is defined as $\oint \vec{f}(\vec{l}).d\vec{l} = \lim_{n \to \infty} \sum_{i=0}^{n} \vec{f}(x_i, y_i, z_i).\delta\vec{l_i}.$  eq(1-7)

This is equal to, $\oint \vec{f}(\vec{l}).d\vec{l} = \lim_{n \to \infty} \sum_{i=0}^{n} |\vec{f}(x_i, y_i, z_i)|.|\delta\vec{l_i}|.\cos(\theta_i).$  eq(1-8)

## 3. Conservative Line Integrals

A line integral is conservative from point $A$ to point $B$, if the final value of the line integral remains constant irrespective of the path of the line selected.

## 4. Surface Area Vector and Functions on a Surface

If $\delta A$ is a small surface area, the Surface Area Vector $\delta\vec{A}$ is defined as the vector with a magnitude which is the same as the surface area $\delta A$ and with the direction perpendicular to the surface area and pointing out of the surface area when $\delta A \to 0$. . Note: Since $\delta A$ is small, it can be assumed to be flat, at the limit.

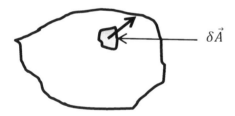

$\delta\vec{A}$

Figure 1-2

A function can be defined on points on a X-Y-Z coordinate system. Hence a function can also be defined on points of a surface, since a surface is simply a restriction on the X-Y-Z coordinate system.

## 5. Surface Integral

Surface Integral of a function is defined by,

$$\oiint \vec{f}(\vec{A}).d\vec{A} = \lim_{n \to \infty} \sum_{i=0}^{n} \vec{f}(x, y, \text{and } z \text{ coordinates of } \delta\vec{A_i}).\delta\vec{A_i}$$  eq(1-9)

Note that function $\vec{f}(x, y, z)$ could very well be a vector in two or three dimensions. In that case $\vec{f}(x, y \text{ and } z \text{ coordinates of } \delta\vec{A_i}).\delta\vec{A_i}$ is the DOT product.

## *Chapter 2:* <u>SYMMETRY OF OBJECTS</u>

1.  Reflective and Rotational Symmetry

Objects such as cylinders, spheres, pyramids, toroids etc., that are of concern to us in AP Physics have at least one of two types of physical symmetry: Reflective Symmetry and/or Rotational Symmetry. Reflective symmetry is that if the object is appropriately cut into two pieces, corresponding pieces are mirror images of each other. Rotational symmetry is if the object is appropriately rotated along an axis, the physical shape of the object remains unchanged.

 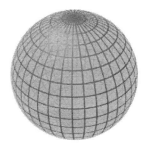 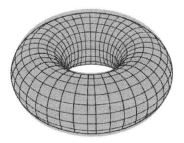

<u>Figure 2-1</u>

2.  Symmetrically Applied Inputs and Resulting Outputs

If we apply vectors such as forces, magnetic fields, electric fields etc., to symmetric objects in a symmetric manner, their resulting outputs maintain symmetry.

In Chapters 3 and 4 we will present several such examples.

# Chapter 3: ELECTRICITY

1. Coulomb's Law

Assume that there are two point electric charges in space denoted by $Q$ and $q$, with $q$ being a test charge used to measure the force induced by $Q$ on a given point in space. If the distance between the electric charges are given by $r$, the force vector $\vec{F}$ between them is directed along the line connecting the two charges, with the direction against the test charge $q$ as follows;

Q .  $\longleftrightarrow$  . q

<u>Figure 3-1</u>

$$\vec{F} = \frac{q.Q}{4\pi\varepsilon_0 r^2}\cdot\frac{\vec{F}}{|\vec{F}|} = \frac{q.Q}{4\pi\varepsilon_0 r^2}\cdot 1_{\vec{F}} \quad N \qquad\qquad eq(3\text{-}1)$$

The magnitude of the force vector is given by,

$$|\vec{F}| = \frac{q.Q}{4\pi\varepsilon_0 r^2} \quad N \qquad\qquad eq(3\text{-}2)$$

The charges $q$, and $Q$ are measured in units of Coulombs (C). (1 C = 1 Ampere . second = 1 As)

Later we will show that *Coulomb's Law* is derivable from *Gauss's Law of Electricity*. However, *Coulomb's Law* is usually easier to use than than *Gauss's Law of Electricity* when dealing with point electric charges and small ($\delta q$) charge segments within a charged volume.

2. Electric Field Strength

If a force $\vec{F}(q)$ is exerted on a point test charge of strength $q$ at a given point in space by one or more other charges, then the Electric Field Strength vector at that point in space is defined as,

$$\vec{E} = \frac{\vec{F}(q)}{q} \quad N/C \qquad\qquad eq(3\text{-}3)$$

The above force consists of the vector addition of all forces due to multiple external charges acting on the point charge $q$.

For Figure 1, the eq(3-3) gives the electric field strength at the point where the charge $q$ is at. This can be calculated from eq(3-1) and eq(3-3) as, $\qquad \vec{E} = \frac{Q}{4\pi\varepsilon_0 r^2}\cdot 1_{\vec{F}} \qquad\qquad eq(3\text{-}4)$

Where the magnitude is given by, $|\vec{E}| = \frac{Q}{4\pi\varepsilon_0 r^2} \quad N/C \qquad\qquad eq(3\text{-}5)$

3. Principle of Superposition for Electric Fields and Force

Principle of Superposition applies for multiple electric charges, with respect to, $\vec{F}$, and $\vec{E}$, in a vacuum. Later we will understand that for other quantities of interest such as potential, electric flux, and magnetic flux in a vacuum this holds true. For most other material media too, this property holds true for practical purposes, except within some types of ferroelectric material.

Hence for multiple point charges of $Q_i$ acting on a test charge $q$, the total force $\vec{F}$ on $q$ is given by,

$$\vec{F} = \sum_{i=1}^{n} \frac{q.Q_i}{4\pi\varepsilon_0 r_i^2} \cdot \frac{\vec{F_i}}{|\vec{F_i}|}$$    eq(3-6)

$$\vec{E} = \sum_{i=1}^{n} \frac{Q_i}{4\pi\varepsilon_0 r_i^2} \cdot \frac{\vec{E_i}}{|\vec{E_i}|}$$    eq(3-7)

4. Observations on Electric Field and Electric Field Lines

| 1 | Electric field lines are imaginary lines used to visualize an electric field, and they are not actual lines in space. |
|---|---|
| 2 | Electric field lines begin and end at an electric charge or at infinity. |
| 3 | Electric field lines have an arrow that point in the direction of the electric field vector $\vec{E}$. |
| 4 | Select a $\delta\vec{A}$ surface, with $\delta\vec{A}$ selected in such a way that the $\delta\vec{A}$ vector is parallel to the electric field at that point in space. Then the density of the number of electric field lines emanating from that surface is equal to the magnitude of the electric field at that surface. |
| 5 | Only one value for $\vec{E}$ exists at a given point in space at a given time, no matter how many charges are there in a given space. The principle of superposition tells us that forces due to individual charges will contribute to, and are components of this vector value $\vec{E}$. |
| 6 | Electric field lines cannot be cut by each other, because $\vec{E}$ is a unique vector at a given point in space at a given time. |
| 7 | If the geometric shape of the container of an electric charge of Q is symmetric, and the charge is distributed symmetrically, the direction and magnitude of $\vec{E}$ is symmetric at symmetric physical points of the container. |
| 8 | If the electric field in two close by points A and B in two different electric field lines have the same magnitude, and approximately the same direction, then there is a line (or surface) in space connecting the two points A and B that require no work to be done on a test charge "q" when the charge is moved from A to B. This line or surface is called an equipotential line (surface). |
| 9 | Given two separate equipotential lines (or surfaces), direction of Electric Field $\vec{E}$ points away from the line(or surface) with the higher potential towards the line (or surface) with the |

| | lower potential. |
|---|---|

## 5. Electric Potential

Electric Potential $V_{A,B}$ is defined as the work $W$ done **by an external entity against an electric field** on a unit positive charge when moving from point A to point B.

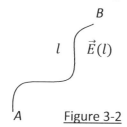

$$\underset{A}{\overset{B}{l \int}} \vec{E}(l)$$

<u>Figure 3-2</u>

$$V_{A,B} = \frac{dW}{dq} \quad Nm/C \qquad \text{eq(3-8)}$$

Note: $1 \frac{N.m}{C} = 1 \frac{J}{C} = 1 \frac{N.m}{A.s} = 1 \frac{J}{A.s} = 1 \frac{W}{A} = 1 A.\Omega = 1 \sqrt{W.\Omega} = 1 \frac{kg.m^2}{C.s^2} = 1 \, Volt$

The work done by an external entity with a point charge of $q$, going from point A to point B, against a charge $Q_i(t)$ in space is given by,

$$W(Q_i(t), q) = -\oint_l \vec{F}(Q_i(t), q).d\vec{l} = -\oint_l q.\vec{E}(Q_i(t)).d\vec{l} \qquad \text{eq(3-9)}$$

Note that the above described work done, is a scalar quantity measured in Joules.

The work done by an external entity with a point charge of $q$, going from point A to point B, when the charges in space at time $t$ are $Q_i(t)$, for $i = 1,2,.. \ n$, is given by the summation of the eq(3-9) over $i$.

By convention, potential at infinity is zero. Potential is also called a Voltage if the potential is measured relative to two points and measured in Joules/Coulomb (=Volt). Sometimes we assume that one point of an electrical circuit has a potential of zero. (For example, potential in the end B of a wire with two ends A and B can be written as $V_B = V_{A,B}$.)

From eq(3-8), at time $t$, $V_{A,B}(t) = \sum_{i=0}^{n} V_{A,B}(Q_i(t)) = -\sum_{i=0}^{n} \frac{W(Q_i(t), q)}{q} \qquad \text{eq(3-10)}$

Hence, $V_{A,B}(t) = -\sum_{i=0}^{n} \oint_l \overrightarrow{E(Q_i(t))}.d\vec{l} = -\oint_l \vec{E}.d\vec{l} \qquad \text{eq(3-11)}$

The electric potential is conservative. As shown in Chapter 1, a conservative line integral is a function whose value does not change, no matter what the path $l$ the path integral takes. The resulting scalar value computed in going from A to B is the same.

For Figure 1, let us orient the X axis along the line connecting the charge $Q$ and $q$, with $Q$ being at the origin of the X axis. Then the above integral gives the potential as shown below,

$$V = V_{\infty,r} = -\int_{x=\infty}^{r} \frac{Q}{4\pi\varepsilon_0 x^2} dx = \frac{Q}{4\pi\varepsilon_0 r} \text{ Volt}$$ eq(3-12)

### 6. Work Done on a Finite Electrical Charge

Work done by an external entity in bringing a charge of $Q$ to point B from a point A (or infinity) is given by,

$$W = \int_0^Q V(q).dq < V(Q).Q$$ eq(3-13)

Note that the act of bringing in the charge $Q$ little by little to point B may itself increase the potential of point B gradually. Hence at the beginning, parts of the charge $Q$ will not encounter the final potential $V(Q)$, and thus the work that needs to be done at the beginning is less.

Further note that when a charge $Q$ is residing in a conductor at a potential $V(Q)$, the eq(3-5) is not applicable, since the assumption of the uniform and symmetric electric field distribution used when deriving eq(3-5) is no longer true for this case. i.e. The presence of the geometric shape of the conductor and electrical properties of the material in the conductor will change the electric fields.

### 7. Gauss's Law of Electricity for Closed Surfaces

Electric Flux over a surface "A" is defined by,

$$\varphi_A = \oiint \vec{E}.d\vec{A} \; Nm^2/C \quad (= \text{Volt.m})$$ eq(3-14)

A

Figure 3-3

Gauss's Law of Electricity states: $\oiint_{A_{closed}} \vec{E}.d\vec{A} = \frac{Q_{closed}}{\varepsilon_0} \; Nm^2/C$ eq(3-15)

### 8. Gauss's Law: Example 1 – Proof of Coulomb's Law via Gauss's Law

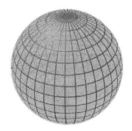

Gaussian surface: A sphere of radius $r$ and the surface area $4\pi r^2$.

A point charge of $q$ is at the center of the sphere.

Figure 3-4

By symmetry, the only direction an electric field can exist on the above Gaussian surface is in the perpendicular direction to the surface. By symmetry the magnitude of the electric field must be the same everywhere on the surface.

Hence using eq(3-15) and evaluating the line integral, we get $\quad |\vec{E}|.\,4\pi r^2 = \frac{q}{\varepsilon_0}$.

Hence the electric field is the same as in eq(3-5).

9.  Gauss's Law: Example 2 - Electric Field in a Long Charged Wire

Let us calculate the electric field caused by a uniformly charged long wire (with no electric current) at a distance $R$ from wire.

Let $\lambda$ be the electric charge density per unit length of wire in units of C/m. Wire has a length $L$.

$\vec{E}$      Gaussian "Pillbox" with radius R, and concentric with the wire

<u>Figure 3-5</u>

By symmetry, only the curved cylindrical surface in the Gaussian "Pillbox" has any electric field coming out, perpendicular to the surface. That electric field is a constant.

Using eq(3-15) and evaluating the surface integral, $\qquad |\vec{E}|.\,2\,\pi\,R\,L = \frac{\lambda\,L}{\varepsilon_0}$

$$|\vec{E}| = \frac{\lambda}{2\,\pi\,R\varepsilon_0} \qquad\qquad\qquad\qquad\qquad\qquad\qquad\qquad \text{eq(3-16)}$$

10. Gauss's Law: Example 3 - Electric Field for a Uniformly Charged Plane

Find the electric field of a uniformly charged plane with charge density σ, by selecting a thin cylindrical surface encompassing a part of the charged plane as a Gaussian "Pillbox".

Prove $|\vec{E}| = \frac{\sigma}{2\varepsilon_0}$ by Gauss's Law of Electricity, for electric fields pointing away from the flat side surfaces of the Gaussian "Pillbox" cylinder, via evaluating the surface integral in eq(3-15).

8

11. Electric Current and Electric Current Density

An electric current is the rate of movement of electric charges across a surface of area $A$. During this movement, all such charges $\delta q$ are identified during a $\delta t$ time period in which the charges emerge out of the surface area $A$. The electric current from the area $A$ is then defined by,

$$i_A(t) = \lim_{\delta t \to 0} \frac{\delta q}{\delta t}$$

eq(3-17)

When the area $A$ above becomes small, it can be considered a flat surface represented by the vector $\delta \vec{A}$. We can then define the current density $\vec{J}$ on that point in the surface by,

$$\vec{J} = \lim_{\delta \vec{A} \to 0} \frac{i_{|\delta \vec{A}|}(t)}{|\delta \vec{A}|} \cdot 1_{\delta \vec{A}}$$

eq(3-18)

Behavior of electric currents vary, depending on the material through which it goes, as shown in the following cases.

a) Case 1: Electric Current coming out of (or going into) a Charge Storage Device

Charge storage devices are equipment such as Van de Graf generators, capacitors, etc., that can accumulate electric charges. In this case, the current coming out of the device is given by selecting a closed surface A that encompasses the device. That current is given by,

$$i(t) = \frac{dQ(t)}{dt}$$

eq(3-19)

where $Q(t)$ is the total charge stored in the device at time $t$.

b) Case 2: Current in a Conductor with Resistance

Let the length of a conducting wire be $l$, with cross sectional area $A$ and with a constant electric potential $V$ at the ends.

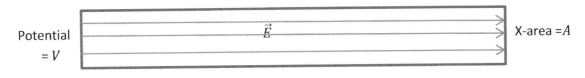

Potential
= V

$\vec{E}$

X-area =$A$

$length = l$

Figure 3-6

$V = -\oint \vec{E}.\,d\vec{l} = |\vec{E}|.\,l$ , follows that $|\vec{E}| = \frac{V}{l}$

Now for an electron with a charge $q = -e,$ force exerted is $|\vec{F}| = |\int \vec{E} \, dq|$ , follows that $|\vec{F}| = \frac{V.e_0}{l}$

Let the speed of an average drifting electron be $v(t)$. Using Newton's 2nd law on the electron, we get,

$m \frac{dv}{dt} = |\vec{F}| = \frac{V.e}{l}$

After an average time of $\tau$ if the electron crashes to an atom and stops its momentum, then by integrating the above equation, the final speed of the electron is $v_\tau = \frac{V.e.\tau}{m.l}$. The average speed can be estimated to be half of that.

If there are $p$ free electrons per unit volume in the metal and the area of the metal is $A$, in 1 second the amount of electrons moved through a cross section area of the wire $= p.A.v_\tau$.

Hence the current in the conductor with resistance at time $t$ is estimated by,

$i(t) = \frac{V.\tau.p.A.e}{2.m.l}$    C/s (1 C/s = 1 A) $\hspace{3cm}$ eq(3-20)

Of course new charges take place of the old charges when old charges drift away to an end of the conductor, due to the continued potential difference. But the net effective charge loss in the conductor is zero.

c)  Case 3: Electric Current in a Vacuum or in a Conductor with No Resistance

When there is no resistance, the $\tau$ in eq(3-20) approaches infinity. Hence from eq(3-20) the only way a finite current can be maintained without resistance is by having a zero potential difference inside the conductor.

Most wires connecting electrical circuit elements can be considered to have a negligible resistance for practical purposes.

d)  Case 4: Electric Current residing inside a permanent magnet

Sustained small circular current loops flow within ferromagnetic material, generating permanent magnetic fields. When magnetized, these loops orient in the direction of magnetization and create a permanent magnet. These current loops tend to disorient over a long period of time based on the nature of the material.

e)  Case 5: Current Residing Inside a Superconductor

The currents inside superconductors tend to stay unimpeded due to a lack of resistance.

f) Case 6: Current in an Object Subject to a Changing Magnetic Field

In this case a current proportional to the rate of change of the magnetic flux is generated. This scenario is explained later under Faraday's Law of Electromagnetic Induction.

12. Electrical Resistance in a Wire and Ohm's Law

Assume that there is an electrically conducting object with a potential difference $V$ and a current $I$ flowing between two of its points. Then the resistance $R$ between the two points of the object is defined as,

$$R = \frac{V}{I} \quad Volts/A \quad (= \Omega)$$ eq(3-21)

Georg Ohm first observed this relationship in thin electric wires and experimentally obtained the value of $R$. Ohm's Law says that the potential is proportional to current. We now know that Ohm's Law works only for a class of electrical devices called resistors.

For the wire in Figure 3-6, with the current described in eq(3-20), the resistance can be computed as,

$$R = \frac{2ml}{\tau.p.A.e_0}$$ eq(3-22)

Note: Resistance is a physical property of the wire dimensions and the material it is made out of. From eq(3-19) we can say, bigger the area of the wire, less is the resistance. Longer the wire, higher the resistance.

The energy $E$, and power $P$, consumed by a resistor when at a steady potential of $V$ with a steady current $I$ is given by,

$$E = W = \int_0^Q V(q,t).dq = V \int_0^Q dq = V.I.t$$ eq(3-23)

$$P = \frac{dE}{dt} = V.I = I^2 R = \frac{V^2}{R}$$ eq(3-24)

13. Capacitance

Capacitance $C$ of a device able to store charges from an electric current $i(t)$ is defined by,

$$C = \frac{Q(t)}{V(t)} = \frac{\int_0^t I(x).dx}{V(t)} \quad \text{(Units = Farad, 1 Farad = 1C/V)}$$ eq(3-25)

The physical mechanism of the capacitive action is excess electrical charge storage. This is equivalent to a time varying current into or out of the capacitor. Compare that to the physical mechanism of the resistor, whose current is generated via the external electric field applied to create electron drift in one direction, without accumulating any excess electrical charge.

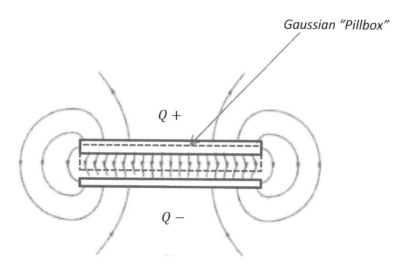

Gaussian "Pillbox"

$Q+$

$Q-$

Figure 3-7

Above is a parallel plate capacitor, with a plate separation of length $d$. Applying the Gauss's Law of Electricity to the above Gaussian "Pillbox", we get the magnitude of the electric field between plates $|\vec{E}| = \frac{Q}{\varepsilon A}$ where $\varepsilon$ is the dielectric constant of the insulating material between the two plates. From the definition of the electric potential line integral, we get, $V = |\vec{E}| \cdot d$.

Hence, $\frac{Q}{\varepsilon A} = \frac{V}{d}$.    Hence, $C = \frac{Q}{V} = \frac{\varepsilon A}{d}$    eq(3-26)

Note: Capacitance depends only on the physical properties of the capacitor. Also, higher the value of the dielectric constant $\varepsilon$ is, higher the amount of charge the capacitor can hold, per Volt of potential applied.

The energy $E$, stored by the capacitor when at a steady potential of $V$ is given by,

$$E = \int_0^{CV} V(q,t).dq = \int_0^{CV} \frac{q}{C} dq = \frac{1}{2} CV^2 = \frac{1}{2} Q.V$$    eq(3-27)

From the above, the energy stored in the capacitor when it is fully charged is $\frac{1}{2} Q.V$. Some people mistakenly assume that the energy stored in the capacitor is $Q.V$ because the charge $Q$ is currently at potential $V$. However they fail to realize that when the first $\delta q$ charge was brought into the capacitor, the potential was zero, so there was no work done on that charge. Each succeeding charge brought in had a successively larger amount of work do, because the charges that were previously brought, made the potential go up.

## Chapter 4: MAGNETISM

1.  Magnetic Fields

    Magnetic fields are vectors. There are two kinds of magnetic fields, the $\vec{H}$ magnetizing field density magnetic field, and $\vec{B}$ flux field density magnetic field. The magnetic fields never start or end, and they form a closed loop. $\vec{H}$ fields are generated by permanent magnets or ferromagnetic material, and $\vec{B}$ fields are generated due to an effect of an electric current.

2.  Definition of the $\vec{B}$ Magnetic Field

    If a point electric charge $q$ travelling in a vacuum through a magnetic field $\vec{B}$ at a velocity of $\vec{v}$, experiences a force of $\vec{F}$ due to the magnetic field, the magnitude and direction of the magnetic field is given by solving the vector equation,

    $$\vec{v} \times \vec{B} = \frac{\vec{F}(q)}{q} \qquad\qquad\qquad\qquad \text{eq(4-1)}$$

3.  Observations on Magnetic Field and Magnetic Field Lines

| 1 | Magnetic field lines have an arrow that point in the actual direction of the magnetic field vector $\vec{H}$ or $\vec{B}$. |
|---|---|
| 2 | Density of magnetic field lines in a $\delta\vec{A}$ surface parallel to the magnetic field is equal to the magnitude of the magnetic field at that surface. |
| 3 | Only one value for $\vec{B}$ or $\vec{H}$ exists at a given point in space at a given time. |
| 4 | Magnetic field lines cannot be cut by each other, because magnetic field is a unique vector at a given point in space at a given time. |
| 5 | There is no concept called "magnetic potential". This is because one cannot do work against magnetic fields using electric charges, since the magnetic field vector generates a force that is always perpendicular to the direction of a travelling electric charge. Further there are no known magnetic "unipoles" existing in nature. |
| 6 | The two types of magnetic fields are indistinguishable in a vacuum. In AP Physics we do not differentiate between the two types of magnetic fields, except when drawing and studying magnetic field lines. |

Units of a magnetic field are called Tesla, for a $\vec{B}$ field. 1 Tesla $= 1\frac{N.s}{C.m} = 1\frac{V.s}{m^2} = 1\frac{kg}{C.s}$

4. Principle of Superposition for Magnetic Fields

The Principle of Superposition always applies to $\vec{B}$ magnetic fields generated by moving electric charges in a vacuum. When $\vec{B}$ magnetic fields go through ferromagnetic material, there is a property called Hysteresis that makes the field behave nonlinearly. That property makes a semi-permanent $\vec{H}$ field (i.e. a permanent magnet.). This makes the principle of superposition not directly applicable for ferromagnetic material. For electric fields in ferroelectric materials, this property applies too, but to a lesser extent.

For example, in Figure 4-1(a) below, we have a piece of cylindrical ferromagnetic material with an insulated electric wire wound around it. When an electric current is increased and decreased in magnitude and direction as shown in Figure 4-1(a), the resulting magnetic field behaves as in Figure 4-1(b).

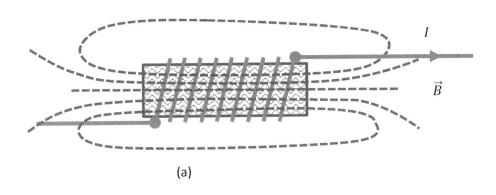

(a)

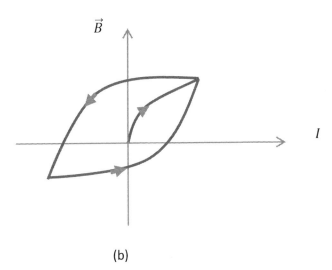

(b)

<u>Figure 4-1</u>

The $\vec{H}$ field is created by small circulating electric current loops inside magnetic material. How the $\vec{H}$ field is generated is similar to the behavior of small solenoids generated from current loops explained later in eq(4-4). When magnetized, the small current loops align themselves in a direction that reinforces their magnetic fields. However, $\vec{H}$ fields are not precisely defined at AP Physics C level.

5.  Ampere's Law of Constant Current

A magnetic field $\vec{B}$ can be induced on a closed loop $l$ with a surface area $A$ whose border is the loop. If the current density in a point in the surface area is $\vec{J}$ (Ampere/$m^2$ ),

Ampere's Law is given by;

$$\oint \vec{B}.d\vec{l} = \mu_0 . \oiint_A \vec{J}.d\vec{A} \quad \text{(N.s/C)} \qquad \text{eq(4-2)}$$

Ampere's Law is true only if the current density coming out of the area $A$ does not vary with time.

In the case of time varying current densities, Maxwell modified this law as shown in Chapter 6.

6.  Ampere's Law Application 1: Magnetic Field from a Current Carrying Wire

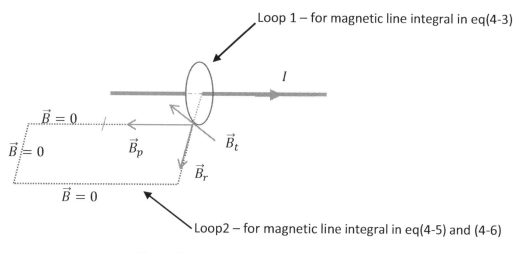

Figure 4-2

Consider a hypothetical circle with radius r, and concentric and perpendicular to the current carrying wire. Due to rotational symmetry of the wire and current, it can be concluded that the magnitude of the magnetic field tangential to the circle $\vec{B}_t$ remains constant when traversing the circle.

If there are any other non zero magnetic field components not tangential to the circle, then they can either be parallel to the wire (call it $\vec{B}_p$), or radial to the wire (call it $\vec{B}_r$).

Now applying Ampere's Law from eq(4-2) to the hypothetical circle, we get,

$$|\vec{B}_t|.2\pi r = \mu_0 I \qquad \text{eq(4-3)}$$

15

Therefore, $\left|\vec{B_t}\right| = \frac{\mu_0 I}{2\pi r}$ $\hspace{4cm}$ eq(4-4)

Assume that the length of wire protruding to the left of the hypothetical circle is given by $l_{lw}$. Assume that the top line of a hypothetical rectangle starts at radial length $r_1$, and the bottom line of the rectangle starts at the radial length $r_2$. By constructing the rectangle shown in Figure 4-2 with left hand side and the bottom side of the rectangle approaching infinity, and applying Ampere's Law from eq(4-2) we get,

$$\left|\vec{B_p}\right|.l_{lw} - \lim_{r_2 \to \infty} \int_{r_1}^{r_2} \text{sign}(\vec{B_r}).\left|\vec{B_r}\right|.dr = 0 \hspace{3cm} \text{eq(4-5)}$$

Where $\text{sign}(\vec{B_r})$ is the sign of the vector $\vec{B_r}$ at radius $r$. The $\vec{B_r}$ is positive when pointing radially outwards from the wire and negative when pointing inwards. Note that due to rotational symmetry, $\vec{B_p}$ must have a constant magnitude until the end of the wire, with the same direction, along the top line of the rectangle in Figure 4-2.

However, the only way the above equation can be true is if $\vec{B_p} = 0$, since for all values of $l_{lw}$ the equation must be true.

Now consider the above rectangle again, but this time without assuming that the radial and axial lengths on left and bottom are close to infinity. Applying Ampere's Law to the rectangle again, we get,

$\int_{r_1}^{r_2} \text{sign}(\vec{B_r}).\left|\vec{B_r}\right|.dr = 0.$ $\hspace{4cm}$ eq(4-6)

However, the only way the above equation can be true for all values of $r_1$ and $r_2$ is by having $\vec{B_r} = 0$.

## 7. Ampere's Law Application 2: Electromagnet

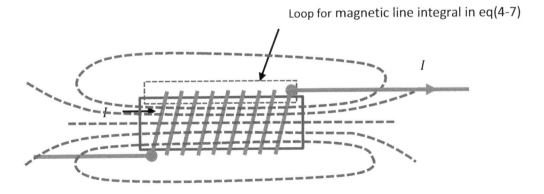

Loop for magnetic line integral in eq(4-7)

Figure 4-3

Consider a solenoid with N turns and length $l$ carrying a steady current $I$ shown in Figure 4-3. Then applying Ampere's Law to the blue dotted rectangle loop gives,

$$|\vec{B}|.l = \mu NI \qquad\qquad\qquad\qquad\qquad\qquad \text{eq(4-7)}$$

Therefore the magnetic field inside the solenoid is given by,

$$|\vec{B}| = \frac{\mu NI}{l} \qquad\qquad\qquad\qquad\qquad\qquad \text{eq(4-8)}$$

8. Biot-Savart Law

Biot-Savart Law says that the magnetic field at a distance $\vec{r}$ generated by a current carrying thin wire segment of length $d\vec{l}$ and current $I$ is given by,

$$d\vec{B} = \frac{\mu_0 \, I \, d\vec{l} \times 1_{\vec{r}}}{4\pi r^2} \qquad\qquad\qquad\qquad\qquad \text{eq(4-9)}$$

Figure 4-4 illustrates the law.

Using this law one can integrate $d\vec{B}$ along the wire and get the value for magnetic field strength caused by the electric current via principle of superposition.

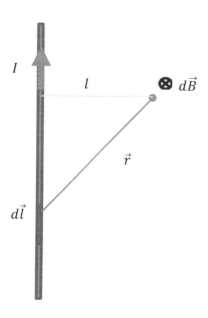

Figure 4-4

Biot-Savart Law is magnetism's equivalent to Coulomb's Law for Electricity. Biot-Savart Law can be proven via Ampere's Law.

Exercise: Use Biot-Savart Law to calculate the magnetic field a distance $r$ away from a long wire with a constant current $I$. (Hint: Sum up the resulting magnetic field from all current elements via the Principle of Superposition and taking into account the sine of the angle between the vectors $d\vec{l}$ and $\vec{r}$.)

Answer: $|\vec{B}| = 2.\frac{\mu_0 I l}{4\pi} \int_0^\infty \frac{1}{l^2+r^2} \frac{l}{(l^2+r^2)^{\frac{1}{2}}} dl = 2.\frac{\mu_0 I l}{4\pi} \int_0^\infty \frac{1}{(l^2+r^2)^{\frac{3}{2}}} dl = \frac{\mu_0 I}{2\pi l}$

Note: The wire above could be bent, and still the above integral is valid, since it does not depend on the geometry of straightness of the wire but only on the length along the wire. By an argument identically in reverse, and using the principle of superposition in reverse, one can show that Biot- Savart Law can be derived from Ampere's Law.

## 9. Lorentz Equation

Forces on a sequence of point particles $i$ $(i = 1, 2, ...., n)$ with an electric charge $q_i$ and velocity $\vec{v}_i$, moving in a magnetic field $\vec{B}_i$ and an electric field $\vec{E}_i$ are given by,

$$\vec{F} = \sum_{i=1}^n q_i.(\vec{E}_i + \vec{v}_i \times \vec{B}_i)$$  eq(4-10)

Lorentz Equation is merely a combination of the definitions for electric field and the magnetic field from eq(3-2), and eq(4-1). Lorentz Equation can also be considered as an alternate definition for electric and magnetic fields in terms of force, electric charge and the velocity of the charge and can replace the definitions in eq(3-2) and eq(4-1).

There is no work done by the magnetic field on charged particles, because the force exerted by the magnetic field is perpendicular to the direction of travel. (Right Hand Rule for Vector Multiplication.)

## 10. Lorentz Equation Example 1: Two Parallel Wires

Consider an electric wire with current $I_1$ and another electric wire with current $I_2$ that is parallel to the first wire, with the current going on the same direction.

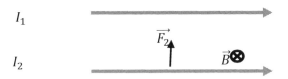

$I_1$

$\vec{F_2}$

$I_2$      $\vec{B}\otimes$

Figure 4-5

If there are $p$ free electrons per unit volume in the wire and the cross sectional area of the wire is $A$, and length of wire is $\vec{l_2}$ measured in the direction of the current, the total amount of free electrons in the wire is = $|\vec{l_2}|.A.p.$

If $v_\tau$ is the drift velocity of electrons and $-e$ is the electric charge in an electron, then by Lorentz Equation in eq(4-5) we get,

$$\overrightarrow{F_{2,B}} = \sum_{i=1}^{n} |\overrightarrow{l_2}| Ap(-e).\overrightarrow{v_\tau} \times \overrightarrow{B_l}$$

From eq(4-4) we know that the magnetic field generated by the 1$^{st}$ wire near the second wire is given by, $|\overrightarrow{B}| = \frac{\mu_0 I}{2\pi r}$.

The electric current in the 2$^{nd}$ wire is given by $I_2 = Ape|\overrightarrow{v_\tau}|$, and we have the force due to the magnetic field given by,

$$\overrightarrow{F_{2,B}} = I_2.\overrightarrow{l_2} \times \overrightarrow{B} \qquad \text{eq(4-11)}$$

Hence, $|\overrightarrow{F_{2,B}}| = I_2.l_2.|\overrightarrow{B}|.\sin(\frac{\pi}{2}) = \frac{\mu_0}{2\pi}\frac{I_1 I_2 l_2}{r}$ \qquad eq(4-12)

Note: From Lorentz Equation, we can see that there is also a force exerted on the 2$^{nd}$ wire, (as well as the first wire due to symmetry) due to the Electric Field $\overrightarrow{E}$ within the 2$^{nd}$ wire, caused due to its potential difference between the ends. But that force is parallel to the 2$^{nd}$ wire along its axis. It has a magnitude of $|\overrightarrow{F_{2,E}}| = \frac{l_2 ApeV}{l_2}$ = $ApeV$, where $V$ is the voltage in the 2$^{nd}$ wire.

## 11. Lorentz Equation Example 2: Direct Current Electric Motor

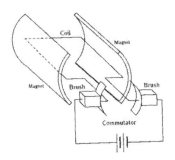

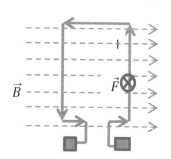

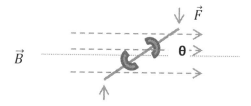

Figure 4-5

From eq(4-11), if the side length of the wire is $l$, and if the vector $\overrightarrow{l}$ is defined in the direction of the current in the side length of the wire, then the force on that piece of wire is given by,

$$\overrightarrow{F} = I\overrightarrow{l} \times \overrightarrow{B} \qquad \text{eq(4-13)}$$

Therefore the torque on the two lengths of wire is given by,

$$\vec{\tau} = 2\vec{r} \times \vec{F} = 2I\vec{r} \times (\vec{l} \times \vec{B})$$

If there is N such loops in the armature of the motor, the total torque is given by,

$$\vec{\tau_N} = 2IN\vec{r} \times (\vec{l} \times \vec{B})$$ 

eq(4-14)

If $A = 2rl$ is the area of the loop (coil), it follows that,

$$|\vec{\tau_N}| = 2INrlB\cos(\theta) = \text{INAB}\cos(\theta)$$ 

eq(4-15)

Hence from eq(4-11) the work $W$ done by the motor after a complete rotation can be calculated by integrating the torque over $\theta$.

$$W = 2\int_{-\frac{\pi}{2}}^{\frac{\pi}{2}}|\vec{\tau_N}|d\theta = 2\int_{-\frac{\pi}{2}}^{\frac{\pi}{2}}INAB\cos(\theta)d\theta = 4\text{ INAB} \quad (\text{Unit = J})$$ 

eq(4-16)

If there are $k$ separate magnets (or electromagnets) in the stator (the non-moving part) of the motor, then from eq(4-10) the work done per rotation of the coil is given by

$$W = 2k\int_{-\frac{\pi}{2k}}^{\frac{\pi}{2k}}INAB\cos(\theta)d\theta = 4k INAB\sin(\frac{\pi}{2k})$$ 

eq(4-17)

If the motor rotates at a frequency of $f$, then the power of the motor $P$ is given by,

$$P = 4fkINAB\sin(\frac{\pi}{2k}) \quad \text{Watts (W)}$$ 

eq(4-18)

Question: As a motor design engineer, find out $k$, the number of magnets needed in the stator that gives out the most power from the motor?

12. Lorentz Equation Example 3: A Particle in a Particle Accelerator

Assuming the mass of a particle charged with a charge $q$ and a travelling with a velocity $\vec{v}$ is given by $m$ in an electric field of $\vec{E}$ and a magnetic field of $\vec{B}$, from Lorentz Equation and Newton's 2nd Law we can write,

$$m.\frac{d\vec{v}}{dt} = q.(\vec{E} + \vec{v} \times \vec{B})$$

Solving the above equation will show that the charge travels in a circle with radius $r$, with speed $v$. Hence

$$m\frac{v^2}{r} = q(|\vec{E}| + v.|\vec{B}|)$$

Pioneering physicist J.J. Thomson in the early 20th century was able to experimentally compute an electron's mass to charge $(e)$ ratio via an equation similar to the following,

$$\frac{m}{e} = \frac{r}{v^2}(|\vec{E}| + v.|\vec{B}|).$$ 

eq(4-19)

Note: Of course at relativistic velocities, these equations are not valid.

## 13. Gauss's Law for Magnetism

The magnetic flux over a surface A is defined by $\Phi_A = \oiint_A \vec{B}.d\vec{A}$

Gauss's Law for Magnetism says, $\oiint_{A \ closed} \vec{B}.d\vec{A} = 0 \quad Nms/C,$          eq(4-20)
for any closed surface $A$.

## 14. Lenz's Law

An induced electromotive force (emf) always gives rise to a current whose magnetic field opposes the original change in magnetic flux.

While Lenz's Law is just a qualitative description of the impact of the changing magnetic flux, above situation, Faraday's Law describes this situation quantitatively.

## 15. Faraday's Law of Electromagnetic Induction

$$\oint \vec{E}.d\vec{l} = -\frac{\partial}{\partial t} \oiint_A \vec{B}\ d\vec{A} \quad Nm^2/C \qquad\qquad eq(4-21)$$

for any closed loop $l$ with $A$ being the surface covering the closed loop.

## 16. Faraday's Law Example: Electric Generator

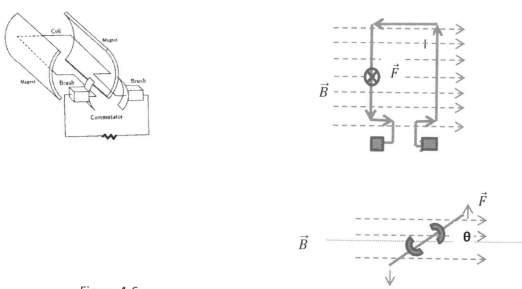

<u>Figure 4-6</u>

Assume that the armature is horizontal at time T=0. At time T= $t$, the angle is given by $\theta = 2\pi f t$.

From Faraday's Law in eq(4-21),

$$V(t) = \frac{\partial}{\partial t}(B.r.l.si\,n(\theta)) = 2\pi f Brl.\cos(2\,\pi f t)$$

Hence the voltage generated is

$$V(t) = 2\pi f Brl.\cos(2\,\pi f t) \hspace{3cm} \text{eq(4-22)}$$

Electricity generators always generate sinusoidal alternate voltage and current internally as shown above. Large generators used by power companies always generate an alternating current based on an equation similar to eq(4-22).

However some generators, by using techniques such as multiple magnets can readjust the start time of the armature to T=0, after a small angle of rotation. These generators can effectively produce an almost direct current.

17. Inductance

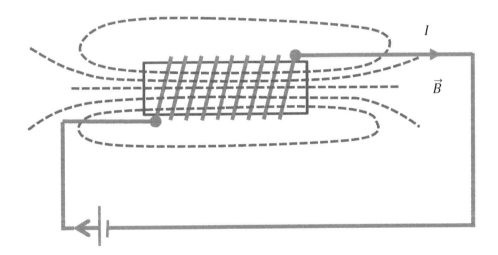

Figure 4-7

If the voltage across a coil of wire is $V(t)$, and the current through the wire is $I(t)$, From Faraday's Law,
$$V(t) = \frac{d}{dt}B(t).A$$

From Ampere's Law, construct a loop for the magnetic field to traverse, identical to that shown in the previous Figure 4-3. Then, $B(t).l = \mu N.I(t)$

Hence, $V(t) = \frac{\mu N A}{l}.\frac{d}{dt}I(t)$

Inductance $L$ of a circuit is defined as, $L = \frac{V(t)}{\frac{d}{dt}I(t)} = \frac{\mu N A}{l}$      eq(4-23)

Note: The inductance is a physical property of the coil.

Energy stored in the magnetic field in the inductor $E$ is given by,

$$E = \int_0^\infty V(t).dq = \int_0^\infty (L\frac{d}{dt}I(t)).I(t).dt = [L(I(t))^2]_0^\infty - \int_0^\infty (L\frac{d}{dt}I(t)).I(t).dt$$

Hence the energy $E$ stored in the inductor $E = \frac{1}{2}LI^2$      eq(4-24)

## *Chapter 5:* ELECTRICAL CIRCUITS

1. Kirchoff's Laws

   a) Sum of all currents coming out of a point in a conductor is zero.

      This is a result of conservation of charge at a point. The net incoming and outgoing charges in a conductor at any point should be zero. Since current is the derivative of charge moved via a surface, the net current outflow from a point should be zero. Hence,

      $\sum_{i=1}^{n} I_i = 0$                                                         eq(5-1)

   b) Sum of potentials in a closed loop of electrical elements is zero.

      This is a result of the definition of potential, and because the potential is conservative. If the point B is identical to point A in Figure 3-2, the evaluated value of eq(3-9) could only be zero. Hence,

      $\sum_{i=1}^{m} V_i = 0$                                                        eq(5-2)

2. Adding R, C, and L Circuit Elements

   It can be easily shown via Kirchoff's Laws and the definition of the voltage current relationship in R, C, and L circuit elements, the following facts:

   a) The combined value $R$ of a group of resistors $R_i$ when connected serially is their algebraic sum. Reciprocal of the combined value of a group of resistors when connected in parallel is the sum of reciprocals of their value.

      *Serial:* $R = \sum_{i=1}^{n} R_i$                                              eq(5-3)

      *Parallel:* $\frac{1}{R} = \sum_{i=1}^{n} \frac{1}{R_i}$                        eq(5-4)

   b) The above rule for resistors holds exactly true for Inductors too.

      *Serial:* $L = \sum_{i=1}^{n} L_i$                                             eq(5-5)

      *Parallel:* $\frac{1}{L} = \sum_{i=1}^{n} \frac{1}{L_i}$                       eq(5-6)

   c) In the case of capacitors, the rules for resisters are reversed with serial taking palace of parallel and parallel taking place of the serial as follows.

      *Parallel:* $C = \sum_{i=1}^{n} C_i$                                          eq(5-7)

      *Serial:* $\frac{1}{C} = \sum_{i=1}^{n} \frac{1}{C_i}$                        eq(5-8)

3.  Transient Behavior of a RC Series Circuit

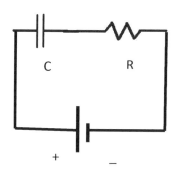

Figure 5-1

If at time t=0 the battery is connected, and a charge q(t) starts building up over time, via Kirchoff's Law of Voltage, we can write,

$V = \frac{dq}{dt} . R + \frac{q}{C}$, with initial conditions $q(0) = 0$                eq(5-9)

Solution to the equation is:  $q(t) = C . V (1 - e^{-\frac{t}{RC}})$                eq(5-10)

Exercise: Write a differential equation for a parallel RC circuit without battery with an initial charge of $Q$, and solve it.

4.  Transient Behavior of a RL Series Circuit

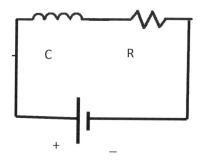

Figure 5-2

If the battery voltage of the above LR series circuit is $V_B$, from Kirchoff's Laws we can write,

$V_B = R \; I(t) + L \frac{d}{dt} I(t)$, with the initial condition $I(0) = 0$.                eq(5-11)

## 5. Alternating Current and Voltage Through Circuit Elements R, C, L

Let us assume that an alternating voltage given by,

$$V(t) = V.\sin(2\pi f t)$$  eq(5-12)

is generated and applied across each of the circuit elements R, C, and L. In the following sections, the resulting current is calculated, and the power consumed is obtained.

a) Resistive element R

From eq( 3-18) and eq(5-4) , the current $I(t)$ through the resistor is given by,

$$I(t) = \frac{V}{R}.\sin(2\pi f t)$$  eq(5-13)

The power $P$ consumed by the resistor using alternating current and voltage are,

$$P = \int_0^{\frac{1}{f}} V(t)\,I(t).\,dt = V.\frac{V}{R}\int_0^{\frac{1}{f}}(\sin(2\pi f t))^2.\,dt. = \frac{V^2}{R}f.\left[\frac{t}{2} - \frac{\sin(4\pi f t)}{8\pi f}\right]_0^{\frac{1}{f}} = \frac{V^2}{2R}$$  eq(5-14)

This is half the energy delivered by a direct current of the same peak magnitude. To compensate for that shortage, the American AC electricity pioneer Nicola Tesla and his British counterpart Sebastian Ferranti called the voltage and current in their newly invented AC generating system *rms* voltage and *rms* Current. This is because Thomas Edison, their rival who had patents for the DC generating system, pointed out that his system gives more power, and tried to monopolize the electric power utilities market in America.

*Rms* stands for Root Mean Square. It is said that Tesla and Ferranti expressed their voltage and current as $V_{rms} = \frac{V}{\sqrt{2}}$, $I_{rms} = \frac{I}{\sqrt{2}}$. Then they cranked up their generator's power output by a factor of approximately 2 by spinning the generator 20% faster at 60Hz, and increasing the peak voltage by about 20% without changing any of their original equipment to achieve the same power output. That is apparently why in Britain the alternating current still has a frequency of 50Hz, while in America it is 60Hz.

b) Capacitive Element C

Differentiating eq(3-22), it can be shown that,

$$I(t) = C.\frac{dV(t)}{dt} = C\frac{d}{dt}V.\sin(2\pi f t) = \frac{CV}{2\pi f}.\cos(2\pi f t)$$

Since $\cos(\theta) = \sin(\theta + \frac{\pi}{2})$, we get,

$$I(t) = \frac{CV}{2\pi f}.\sin(2\pi f t + \frac{\pi}{2})$$  eq(5-15)

The Figure 5-3 below illustrates how the voltage lags the current by 90 degrees.

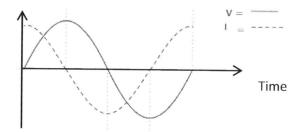

Time

Figure 5-3

The power $P$ consumed by the capacitor using alternating current and voltage are,

$$P = \int_0^{\frac{1}{f}} V(t)\, I(t).\, dt = V.\frac{CV}{2\pi f} \int_0^{\frac{1}{f}} \sin(2\pi ft).\cos(2\pi ft).\, dt. = 0 \qquad \text{eq(5-16)}$$

This is truly the answer we should expect, since the capacitor does not consume power, but stores it as shown in eq().

c)  Inductive Element L
    From eq(4-19) it can be shown that,

$$I(t) = \frac{1}{L} \int_0^t V(x).\, dx = \frac{V}{2\pi fL}\, [-\cos(2\pi fx)\,]_0^t = \frac{V}{2\pi fL}\, (1 - \cos(2\pi ft))$$

Since from trigonometry we know that $-\cos(\theta) = \sin\left(\theta - \frac{\pi}{2}\right)$, the current is given by,

$$I(t) = \frac{V}{2\pi fL}\, \left(1 + \sin\left(2\pi ft - \frac{\pi}{2}\right)\right) \qquad \text{eq(5-17)}$$

As in the case of the capacitor, the power consumption of the inductor is zero, since all energy in the inductor is stored in its magnetic field.

The Figure 5-4 below illustrates how the voltage leads the current by 90 degrees.

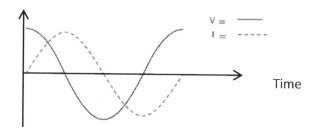

Time

Figure 5-4

# *Chapter 6:* MAXWELL'S EQUATIONS

### 1. Integral Form of Maxwell's Equations

There are 4 Maxwell's Equations.

The integral form of Maxwell's equations are as follows:

(i)     Gauss's Law of Electricity: $\oiint_{A_{closed}} \vec{E}.d\vec{A} = \frac{Q_{closed}}{\varepsilon_0} \quad Nm^2/C$

(ii)    Gauss's Law of Magnetism: $\oiint_{A\ closed} \vec{B}.d\vec{A} = 0 \quad Nms/C$

(iii)   Faraday's Law of Induction: $\oint \vec{E}.d\vec{l} = -\frac{\partial}{\partial t} \oiint \vec{B}\ d\vec{A} \quad Nm/C$

(iv)    Ampere's Law as modified by Maxwell: $\oint \vec{B}.d\vec{l} = \mu_0 . \oiint_A \vec{J}.d\vec{A} + \frac{1}{c^2}\frac{\partial}{\partial t} \oiint_A \vec{E}.d\vec{A} \quad Ns/C$

First three of the above equations were investigated in Chapters 3 and 4. However Ampere's Law is valid only for steady currents. Maxwell modified Ampere's Law to include currents that vary in time, and came up with the fourth equation.

### 2. Electromagnetic Wave Propagation

Assuming a coordinate system of X-Y-Z, it can be shown that an electric field and a magnetic field propagating forward in the direction X is consistent with Maxwell's Equations, if the fields are described by the functions below,

$$\vec{E}(x,t) = \vec{1}_Z \cdot E \sin(2\pi f \left(t - \frac{x}{c}\right)) \qquad\qquad eq(6\text{-}1)$$

$$\vec{B}(x,t) = \vec{1}_Y \cdot E \sqrt{\frac{\varepsilon_0}{\mu_0}} \sin(2\pi f \left(t - \frac{x}{c}\right)) \qquad\qquad eq(6\text{-}2)$$

The $\vec{1}_Y$, and $\vec{1}_Z$ are the unit vectors in the direction of Y and Z axes. $E$ is the maximum possible magnitude of the electric field. This can be proven by constructing a rectangular area of length $\frac{c}{f}$ that travels forward along the X direction at a velocity of $c$, and checking the validity of the four Maxwell's Equations above.

From eq(6-1) and (6-2) it can be shown that the two magnetic and electric fields will move in the X direction at the speed of light $c$. Light, radio waves, X-rays, ultraviolet rays, gamma rays, microwaves, and infrared radiation are all such waves.

## *Chapter 7:* IMPORTANT ITEMS TO REMEMBER

1. Coulomb's Law $|\vec{F}| = \frac{q.Q}{4\pi\varepsilon_0 r^2}$ N

2. Electric Field Strength defined via a test charge $q$: $\vec{E} = \frac{\overrightarrow{F(q)}}{q}$ N/C

3. Electric Potential from point $A$ to point $B$ can be interpreted in 3 ways:

$$V_{A,B}(t) = \sum_{i=0}^{n} V_{A,B}\left(Q_i(t)\right) = -\sum_{i=0}^{n}\oint_l \overrightarrow{E\left(Q_i(t)\right)}.d\vec{l} = -\oint_l \vec{E}.d\vec{l}$$

Nm/C (1Nm/C = 1 Volt)

4. Gauss's Law of Electricity: $\oiint_{A_{closed}} \vec{E}.d\vec{A} = \frac{Q_{closed}}{\varepsilon_0}$ $Nm^2/C$

5. Kirchoff's Laws: Sum of all currents in to a conductor (such as connecting wire in a circuit) is zero. Sum of voltages in a closed loop in an electrical circuit is zero.

6. Resistance: $R = \frac{V(t)}{I(t)}$, Capacitance: $C = \frac{\int_0^t I(x)dx}{V(t)}$, Inductance: $L = \frac{V(t)}{\frac{d}{dt}I(t)}$.

7. Energy of an Electrical System:

Resistor: $VIt = I^2Rt$ (Energy consumed), Capacitor: $\frac{1}{2}CV^2$ (Energy stored in electric field) Inductor:

$\frac{1}{2}LI^2$ (Energy stored in magnetic field) $Nms$

8. Magnetic Field Strength defined via a test charge $q$: $\vec{v} \times \vec{B} = \frac{\overrightarrow{F(q)}}{q}$

9. Units of the $\vec{B}$ magnetic field: Ns/Cm

10. Ampere's Law: $\oint \vec{B}.d\vec{l} = \mu_0 . \oiint_A \vec{J}.d\vec{A}$ $Ns/C$

11. Lorentz Equation: $\vec{F} = \sum_{i=1}^{n} q_i.(\vec{E_i} + \vec{v_i} \times \vec{B_i})$ N

12. Gauss's Law of Magnetism: $\oiint_{A\,closed} \vec{B}.d\vec{A} = 0$ $Nms/C$

13. Faraday's Law of Electromagnetic Induction: $\oint \vec{E}.d\vec{l} = -\frac{\partial}{\partial t}\oiint \vec{B}\,d\vec{A}$ Nm/C

14. Alternating Current and RMS

15. RC, LR, LC, and RL circuits in series and in parallel with and without a battery

16. Maxwell's Equations

The author obtained his bachelor's degree with first class honors in Electronic and Telecommunications Engineering from University of Moratuwa, Sri Lanka in 1982, and a PhD from University of California, Berkeley in 1989. This booklet stemmed from the author's attempt to utilize his many years of experience in teaching, research, and industry in electrical engineering and computer science to make AP Physics C students clearly and accurately understand the required concepts in electricity and magnetism.